Looking 4 Truths
Using Zen and Mindfulness to Transform Your Life

Zen Mister Series
Volume II

Zen Master Bub-In
Peter Taylor

Contents

Introduction
The Four Outrageous Claims	vii

Truth 1 - THERE IS SUFFERING   1

So It Hurts	2
What Do You Expect?	4
Rock Bottom	5
Addressing Depression	6
Self-Improvement	8
The Second Step	10
No Problem	11
Reset	13
Courage	15
Even You	16
Just Passing Time	18
It's OK Now	19
Something to Smile About	20
Distraction	21
Feeling Stupid	22
Expressing Anger	24
Welcoming Anxiety	26
Befriending Loneliness	27
Please Don't Feed the Beast	29
Transform Your Emotions	31

Truth 2 - THERE IS A CAUSE OF SUFFERING 33

Zen Ideas	34
You Think You Think	36
The Simple Truth	37
Logic, Faith, Joy	38
Self Pity	39
Timing Is Everything	41
Beautiful People	43
Holding Happiness	45
Giving Up and Letting Go	46
Pass the Rock	48
The Real World	49
Delightful Delusion	50
Consciousness, Intelligence and the Universe	51
One Thing or Another	53
Death Practice	54
No-Self Esteem	55
Believe In Yourself	57
Self-Worth	58
What Do You Want?	59
The Freedom of Zen	60

Truth 3 - THERE IS A CURE FOR SUFFERING — 61

Something Possible	62
Buddha Did It	63
Wild Horses	64
Your Best Friend	66
Resistance Is Futile	67
You're So Cute When You're Asleep	69
When We Were Babies	70
Growing Up	72
Life and Death	74
Born Again Zen	75
Certain Doubt	76
Just Now	77
Imagine Happiness	78
What Matters	79
Size Matters	80
Are We There Yet?	81
It Could Be Great	82
Shift Happens	83
Turning the Tide	84
Mind Swap	86
The Plunge	87

Truth 4 - THERE IS A WAY TO THAT CURE — 89

End of Suffering	90
Regulating Emotions	91
Breathe Deeply	93
Two Paths	94
Ten Wonderful Things	96
Serve or Observe	98
Observing and Serving	100
Big Ideas	102
Mindful Moments	103
Liar Liar	105
Butterflies	107
Hocus Focus	108
Expect Nothing	109
Pleasure and Pain	110
Feeling the Rain	111
Being Pain	112
Mood Addictions	113
Rethinking Relapse and Recovery	115
Brainwashing	116
You are Here	117
Groovy Ruts	118
Ace in the Hole	119
Drunk Meditation	120
Self-Deprivation Meditation	121
The Spiritual Grind	123
Finding Peace	124

Afterthought	125
About The Author	126
About the Artist	127
About Inroads Press	127

Introduction

The Four Outrageous Claims

The Four Noble Truths are the basis of Buddhist philosophy. They state that 1, there is suffering, 2, there is a cause of suffering, 3, there is a cure for suffering, and 4, there is a way to that cure. These simple statements have profound implications. That is, if they are true.

That there are even Four Noble Truths is quite a claim. "Four" is relatively simple, "noble" and "truth" are complicated. To deal these complicated words we can look at them in their historical context. As the basis of a major world religion, which grew out of feudal societies, calling the Buddha's insights into the nature of life, "the Four Noble Truths" had great marketing appeal. Calling these insights "the Four Outrageous Claims" would more accurately describe the skepticism of the Zen process, but it probably would not have inspired as much confidence in as many people.

The primary goal of a Buddhist practice is to save all beings from suffering. The Buddha believed that understanding these truths would help people escape their suffering. In order to simplify things for the people and to get them started on the path, the Buddha presented his findings as truths. Also, he believed them to be true from his direct experience. To distinguish these important truths from ordinary truths and to impress people, who generally lived as subjects to kings, he added the word noble. Finally, he counted the statements and came up with the number four.

Four, you can trust. You can count the statements for yourself. Four is true, but that is a common truth. A truth such as there is cure to suffering could be considered noble in comparison. So noble is also true. If we can comprehend "four" and "noble" then all we have left to understand is the "thruths". That is a tall order. In order to understand the truth of the "truths" we have to cure suffering. That is the work of a lifetime or more.

To look into the truth of the Four Noble Truths, you have to look for yourself and see suffering. You have to recognize a cause of suffering. Then, you have to take on faith that there is a cure, while you practice the way to that cure. The practice of Zen and mindfulness is following that way and putting the four noble truths to the test.

Looking 4 Truths is a companion to you on that search for truth. It is a series of essays organized around the Four Noble Truths, that help you look into your own experiences of suffering and joy in order to facilitate change in your life. The first section contains writings about the ways that we suffer. The second section discusses causes for our suffering. The third section has essays that consider the possibility of a cure for suffering. The fourth section talks about meditation and mindfulness practices that represent the way to that cure.

The Zen practice of mindfulness does not rely on an in-depth understanding of Buddhist philosophy, it relies on basic awareness of your everyday experience. If you have not been exposed to many Buddhist ideas, this book will provide fresh perspectives, and possibly some insights into your experience. If you are a seasoned Buddhist practitioner or scholar, this book will amuse you and inspire a renewed dedication to practice. This book cannot prove or disprove the truth for you. That, you have to do for yourself. Look into it.

Truth 1

There Is Suffering

There once was a suffering guy,
Who gave meditation a try.
He sat and he sat
On his cushion and mat
And his mind opened up like the sky.

So It Hurts

One way to get through negative emotions is to feel negative emotions. A lot of times, when we start to feel a bit down, the end of the world seems to loom on the horizon. The negative emotion gets immediately amplified. When we feel sick, we think we may die. When somebody breaks up with us, we think we are unlovable and will be lonely forever. In order to avoid this amplified negativity, we need to stay rooted in the present moment and feel just what we are feeling. The feeling is not so bad if we don't make it worse.

If we are feeling negative and we look into the future, we will see doom and gloom. If we look into the past, we will find regrets. If we stay present and feel our current emotion, we will experience a bit of pain. When we stop to feel the pain, breathe in and out with the pain, we see that we can endure the pain. We gain strength and wisdom as we explore the pain.

We generally hate to feel pain. When we start to feel pain, we retreat into our thoughts. Our thoughts though, feed the pain. We start to make sweeping generalizations about ourselves that have no basis in truth. They are based in pain. We start to think we are stupid, ugly, naive, unlucky, lazy, or horrible. This is where our thoughts lead us when we try to avoid the pain of a negative emotion. It's far better just to feel the pain.

When we get used to feeling the pain and see that our emotional experience does not make or break us, we learn to experience subtleties in our emotions. We can interrupt some of our automatic responses and save ourselves from jumping to anger when we really feel hurt or scared. Emotions are amazing. So they hurt sometimes. When we learn to feel just how they hurt, they don't hurt so much. When we can pay close attention to our emotions, we become sages, not victims.

What Do You Expect?

Buddha sets the bar pretty low when he says that life is suffering. That's what you can expect. If you expect to suffer, you will be constantly surprised by joy and pleasures.

When you expect to suffer and then you suffer, it isn't so horrible because that is just what you were expecting. If you are fortunate enough to suffer only a little bit, you may feel grateful because you were expecting to suffer a lot.

If you expect endless pleasures, then the suffering will really sneak up on you. When you expect only pleasantness and find yourself suffering, you may think something is terribly wrong with you. If you notice that you're only having a little bit of fun, you may not enjoy it at all because you think that you should be having a lot of fun. In that case, your little bit of fun turns into suffering.

If you expect to suffer, you do not invite suffering, you just recognize it when it happens. You wake up one day and you are sick, so you take a rest and drink some juice. You think that even though you are normally so good to your body, you became sick, just as you knew you would. You try not to worry too much that you were expecting to go to Disney World that day.

Rock Bottom

Rock bottom is a comforting idea. If we imagine that there is a rock bottom, we can deal with anything. We would know that we can only go down so far and we will find something solid at last.

Unfortunately, we tend to think that things can always get worse. This sense of things getting worse worries us even when we are no where near rock bottom. Things may be pretty good for us. We may have food to eat, people who love us, a warm bed to sleep in, yet we still imagine that things might get worse and the thought makes us uneasy.

Rock bottom does not exist. That may seem like bad news if you are on a steady decline and you want to stop, but it is excellent news if you are plummeting. We are all falling and falling and how we manage the fall is up to us. If we are falling and imagine a rock bottom, then we fall in fear. If we know there is no bottom, we fall in freedom. When we are falling, we are weightless. Anything is possible.

Addressing Depression

There is a little comfort in the idea depression is a disease and not lifestyle choice. Nobody is to blame for becoming depressed. Nobody in their right mind would choose to be depressed. Nobody who is depressed is exactly in their right mind either. Being depressed makes it more difficult to make the type of choices that can lead you out of depression, but there are things that you can do to address your depression.

The depression lives somewhere between body and mind. The body elements of depression are things like hormones, which are influenced by diet and sleep and exercise. Placing your depression in your body makes it seem more like a sickness, like the flu. It will pass if you drink plenty of fluids and get rest.

The part of depression that is in the mind is scarier because we tend to associate ourselves closely with our minds. We think that if there is a problem with our mind, then there is a problem with us. We are not really our minds any more than we are our bodies. We are both and something else. We are something that can recognize that we are suffering from depression and can look for causes and solutions to that suffering. Although we can't just choose to be happy, we can choose to try things that will set the stage for our happiness. We can recognize our situation, do what we can to address the situation and ask for help when we need it.

Self-Improvement

We believe that there is always room for self-improvement. That is not true. That belief is a natural response to our basic state of discontent. When we live our lives through our egos and feel the essential suffering of life, we cannot help but imagine that we could be better people. We could be stronger, smarter, faster, better looking, happier, nicer, or more enlightened. Changes in our circumstances do not improve us, they just change how we imagine ourselves.

We live in a world that is centered around us. We see out of our eyes and we walk on our feet. We develop an idea about who we are that is constantly measured against some ideal that we are not. We see beautiful, admirable characteristics in people all around us and we want to possess those characteristics. We imagine that if we possessed those characteristics, our discontent would go away. We imagine that, because we do not possess those characteristics, we are not as good as we could be. We either feel despair that we cannot experience the ease of life that others seem to enjoy, or we constantly feed the desire to improve ourselves.

If we stop feeding the desire for self-improvement and take a good look at what and who we are, we can appreciate our circumstances as they are. When we understand that we are not our circumstances, that understanding will not improve us or diminish us, it will just mark another step in our journey.

If we don't worry about becoming smarter, happier, and nicer, we give our intelligence, joy and kindness the opportunity assert themselves. When our joy and kindness express themselves in all that we do, the universe will not improve, it will just continue to flow, changing and changing.

The Second Step

    The first step is admitting that you have a problem. Figuring out what your problem is is much more difficult. Deciding what to do about your problem is a whole other problem. The first step is easy. Is everything in your life perfect? No? So you have a problem.
    To figure out what your problem is, you have to look at yourself. Any problem not rooted in you is not your problem. If you think that your problem is your mother, father, friend, lover, job, school, or world affairs, then you have not identified your problem. If you think that your problem is physical or emotional pain then that may seem like a problem that is truly rooted in you and therefore your problem, but that's not exactly your problem either.
    As you continue to figure out what your problem is, you have to decide what to do about the pain and world affairs. When you figure out what your problem is, then your life will be perfect. You may still experience physical and emotional pain and encounter difficulties with your friends, family and world affairs, but you will no longer have a problem.

No Problem

We all think we have problems. Problems are the bane of our existence. What would we do without problems? We would live happily ever after.

The problem with problems is that they keep coming. As soon as we get done with a problem, we move on to the next problem. This habit is problematic.

However, we love solving problems. We create games that are carefully constructed problems for us to solve. Basketball is basically the problem of getting a ball to go through a hoop. If you have the ball, the opposing team creates problems for you in your attempts to solve the ball and hoop problem. The rules also create problems. If you are holding the ball, you can't even walk unless you bounce it. If you stop bouncing the ball, then you can't walk at all, that's it. Problems, problems, problems.

Our problems are not a game. Our problems are serious, but even our serious problems are thrilling to solve. When we fix our problem of loneliness by falling in love we are ecstatic. Of course, love creates more problems. When we are lonely though, we welcome the problems of love. When we are having love problems, we think we have real problems and we start to think that our lonely problems were not so bad.

Problems are what we make of them. The difference between a real problem and a fun problem is our feeling. When you recognize that you can handle any situation, then problems become opportunities for awareness. When you encounter a problem, you can explore your fear, your anxiety, your anger, your feelings. When you can address those, you can handle anything. Without these feelings, your problem is just a situation. No problem.

Reset

Bad moods become depression when they linger for days or weeks or years. Depression is horrible. When you get stuck in depression, all the happy faces in the world won't make you smile. If you do manage to smile through your mood, it is a hollow smile, just being polite for others. If you are unfortunate enough to fall into that pit, then you could use a reset button.

We don't have a reset button. There is a reset practice though. The most difficult part of practice is beginning. When you are depressed, making yourself do anything can be difficult. The good thing about the reset practice is that it is essentially doing nothing. The practice is meditation. Daily meditation can lift you out of depression and then it really starts to work.

It is most difficult to sit when you are depressed, because it is so difficult to focus. If you keep practicing your focus will improve. Slowly, your mood will improve. When you have meditated your way out of your depression, then daily meditation will work as a daily reset. If you are suffering from insomnia, you can get up and meditate, reset and go to sleep. If you wake up in the morning feeling nervous you can meditate, reset and face your day. If you have had a tough day, you can meditate, reset, and enjoy your evening. If you are feeling good, you can meditate, reset and continue to feel good.

Meditation works because it gets you beyond your thoughts. When your thoughts stop, you reset. Clean slate, fresh start, beginners mind, reset.

Courage

Courage is action despite fear. Everyday, we act courageously. Speaking through shyness is an act of courage. Getting out of bed in the morning and facing the day can take tremendous courage. Telling the truth to a friend takes a lot of courage. Writing an answer on a test requires courage. The more fear and insecurity you have, the more courage you display in your activities.

We are all afraid. Fear is common. Fortunately, courage is abundant. When you recognize how much courage you have, you don't have to worry so much about your fears. Each fear that you experience with awareness presents an opportunity to be courageous. If you do not pay attention to your fear, you just feel afraid and the fear can paralyze you. When you notice your fear and remember how courageous you are, you can do what you need to do despite fear.

Courage is held in high esteem in society. People come to think of it as an attribute of rare heroes, who put their lives on the line for the benefit of others. Courage should be held in high esteem. It is an attribute of all of us, which allows us to function in a scary world. If we practice being mindful of our worries and fears, we will notice how incredibly courageous we are everyday.

Even You

It seems like depression is personal. It is a problem that has chosen to bring you down while everybody else seems capable of enjoying life. Other people smile naturally. They enjoy the small things and the big things. Other people have fun easily. You, however, have something wrong with you. Your particular situation makes enjoying life impossible. Happiness is simply not an option for you.

Even you are capable of finding enjoyment in life. Even in your particular situation, you can change your mind and change your world. The only idea you need to change is that your situation is unworkable. Change the idea that there is something particular about you that makes pleasure impossible. If you think that about you, then your idea of you is as big as the moon.

You are not as big as the moon. You are quite small compared to the moon. You're idea of yourself is distorted. You are suffering from a distorted idea of yourself. You are not so special that you are the only human being incapable of happiness. You are so special because, despite what you are going through, even you are capable of finding joy in life.

You are extra special, because when you do find your way to joy, you will become a beacon of light to help others who will feel like you do now. Hang in there. Howl at the moon.

Just Passing Time

When life feels difficult, just passing time is an achievement. When life feels easy, time just passes and achievements happen along the way. Time is the same.

Time passes. We pass time. We take our time. We spend time. We share our time. We run out of time. We need more time. We don't have enough time. We have too much time. We make our time count. We waste time. We want something to show for our time. We have good times and bad times.

That we can try to possess time, shows how we will grasp onto anything. Time is only a reflection of us. Time flies or drags depending on our moods. It moves according to our awareness. If we feel oppressed by time, we are oppressed by our feelings. Time is a great mirror of awareness. We project our impressions onto time, but time is nothing. You can't feel time, you can't see time, you can't smell time, but it seems to leave a trail.

When we find ourselves willing time to speed up or slow down, we are noticing our suffering. We are wishing for things to be just a bit (or a lot) other than they are. That is us, just passing time.

It's OK Now

You are fine. No matter what you think may be wrong, you will get through this. If you are reading these words, then your life is totally manageable. Whatever you have been through is in your past. Whatever you are anticipating is in the future. The past and future are only your imagination. Right now is all that is real. Right now, you are reading. Breathe in deeply. When you exhale, feel relief. If you breathe in again, then you are still alive. Rejoice.

You can have all kinds of complex issues, but as long as you can breathe in and out, you can deal with anything. Things are just as they are and they are perfect that way. You are perfectly placed in the world.

It is not easy to let go of your problems, but it is far more difficult to carry them with you. Now is when you are. Now is simple. Look, listen, feel and breathe. It's all ok. It's even a little bit wonderful. Peace.

There Is Suffering

Something to Smile About

There is always something to smile about. Even when you are feeling your lowest, you are capable of experiencing something delightful and slipping into a genuine smile. It is fairly common to laugh through tears. If you are feeling a lot of pain or distress, that something that makes you smile can be a welcome reminder of your basic joy.

If you don't think that you have anything to smile about, think again. If you still don't have anything to smile about, then stop thinking.

Smiles are like water and air. You need one every so often. Fortunately, no matter where you are, if your unsmiling mood lasts too long, your face will find something to smile about. If you notice your face smiling, enjoy.

Distraction

All we ever want is to be distracted. If you are content just being in the moment, you will not seek distraction. You may feel love, but you won't long for love. Longing for love is wishing for a distraction. Without the distraction you just feel you. That feeling of you may feel like loneliness, so you dream up another person to come and distract you. You imagine that person will adore you and you will adore them. You will snuggle and cuddle and laugh and play. What a wonderful distraction that fantasy is. What a wonderful distraction that person would provide.

As you get into a relationship you get caught up in the distraction and it becomes a part of you. It may not go as you hoped and instead of becoming a pleasant distraction, it becomes a source of pain. You soon need a distraction from your distraction.

Hopes, dreams and plans, provide all kinds of distractions. Imagining better circumstances is a regular occupation. Striving is inviting distraction. To stop inviting distraction, you don't need to stop striving; you need to be present. If you recognize when you are seeking a distraction, you can be present in that distraction and it becomes your focus. When you give up on the idea that there is a better time than now, you can stop reaching for distractions and contentedly engage opportunities.

Feeling Stupid

It's a terrible feeling to feel stupid. We put such a high value on intelligence that if you start to suspect that you're stupid, you are filled with shame. The irony is that the stupidest people never suspect that they are stupid. If you suspect that you are stupid, you are surely intelligent. If you think that you might be stupid and explore that thought a bit, then you are using introspection to confront a deeply held fear. That is a wise thing to do. If you think that you are intelligent and you pride yourself on your intelligence, you may actually prevent yourself from learning, because you think you already know things.

Starting from stupid, is the best way to learn. There is no pride in stupid. If you let yourself be stupid, you will be open to learning anything you don't know. People who think they are smart and know more than you may snigger at you if you ask a question about something that seems obvious to them. In that situation, you are being smart, expanding your knowledge with an honest question, and the sniggerer is being ignorant, blowing up their ego and causing another human pain.

What we think we know usually gets in the way of actually knowing. There is no greater knowledge than knowing what you don't know. If you want to improve yourself, work on being kind.

Work on being confident. Follow your curiosity. Feeling stupid is a feeling, being stupid is believing that feeling. Accepting stupid is a gateway to wisdom.

Expressing Anger

Anger is an emotion that requires careful expression. Any thoughtless expression of anger can easily turn anger into violence. Becoming violent does not address the cause of the anger, it just spreads the problem to the people nearest to you. The root of anger is fear and hurt. If you express your anger, letting it become violence, you take the fear and hurt that you are feeling and inflict it on those around you. The people subject to your anger will be hurt by you and afraid of you and they will also become angry. That is how anger spreads.

Anger creates a pressure, which wants to be released. When you feel that pressure you should treat it like a lit stick of dynamite and take it to a wide open space to blow up safely. Once you are safely out of range of others, you can defuse the bomb instead of letting it explode. If you feel angry, you can look into your situation to see why you are hurt and what is scaring you. If you figure out why you are so upset, you can talk to somebody about it and let them know just how and why you are hurting. Then things actually get better.

If when you feel anger, you just vent your anger, without considering those around you, they will not bother to notice that you are afraid and hurt. They will become defensive rather than compassionate. If you use your anger to help you notice how you hurt, you will find ways to stop hurting and the people around you will help you. Anger does not need to be expressed, but it needs to be released. With a mindful approach to your anger, you can transform it into compassion instead of violence. Everybody will feel better then.

Welcoming Anxiety

We welcome good moods naturally. Bad moods are harder. Bad moods are teachers and we have to learn to welcome them so we can learn from them. In order to welcome a mood, you have to separate the mood from the story of the mood. If you feel anxious, you have to welcome anxiety.

The unwelcoming attitude is thinking, *I am anxious because…* The welcoming attitude is thinking, *I am fine, wonderful, perfect, but I am feeling anxious now.* When you recognize that your anxiety is not going to carry you away, you can lean into it. If you meditate, then meditate with it. If you don't meditate, you can still sit and feel where the anxiety sits in your body. You can focus on that place and breathe. If you find yourself thinking about why you are anxious, then recognize your thoughts and return your focus to your feeling of anxiety. You can also do this lying down, or in a bath, or in the car. You will feel your anxiety recede, and you will be left with the understanding that you are fine.

When the anxiety comes back, as it always does, welcome it, and learn from it again.

Befriending Loneliness

If you find yourself feeling lonely, it is the perfect time to find yourself. Loneliness is the basic suffering of life. It is the fundamental discomfort of being alone with yourself. It is confronting your core discontent. Friends and lovers can't rescue you from loneliness. They can only distract you. Loneliness will continue to seek you out until you make friends with it.

To make friends with loneliness, you have to welcome the feeling. Although it is an uncomfortable feeling, it is there to show you something wonderful about yourself. When you notice loneliness, you can neither give in to it, nor run away from it. You have to confront it. If you give in to it, you will feel miserable and imagine a long sad life ahead of you. You will imagine that you have personal deficits that make loneliness inevitable for you.

If you run away from it, you will do all kinds of frivolous things to keep yourself busy and distracted. You can develop all kinds of habits to keep loneliness at bay, but the feeling will wait for you. It will be there for you until you face it and find out that wonderful thing about yourself.

To find that wonderful thing, you have to ask your loneliness what is so wonderful about you. Then make a list. If the loneliness remains, add to your list. Keep adding to your list until you find that specific wonderful thing that the loneliness is trying to tell you about. Don't doubt for a second that you will find it, but be patient. Every time you feel lonely, look again. Soon you will find yourself and you will have your loneliness to thank. Your loneliness will be gone, but you will have parted as friends.

Please Don't Feed the Beast

When you suffer from anxiety, it is like there is a hungry beast living in the pit of your stomach. If you want it to go away, you have to stop feeding it. The beast feeds on your thoughts, on your fear and worry. You may wonder how the beast came to be. Did your thoughts awaken the beast or did the beast awaken on its own and begin creating food for itself with your thoughts? If the beast is awoken by your worries, then you need to be careful about indulging your imagination by thinking about the future, or trying to guess what somebody else is thinking about you. If the beast is invoking your thoughts, then the worry came first and you are projecting your worry onto something in your environment. Considering that question is more important than finding an answer. Either way, you have to deal with the beast.

The beast feeds on your thoughts, so you have to stop feeding it. To cut off your thinking you start by observing your thoughts. See what you are worrying about. Maybe say it out loud to get it out in the open. Then breathe in deeply into your stomach. Wag your chin around to see if there is tension in your jaw, then breathe out. Focus your attention on your breath so there is no extra room for thoughts. If a thought sneaks in, observe it. If it is doom and gloom, it is food for the beast. Breathe it out. Keep breathing mindfully until you have lulled the beast to sleep.

The less food you prepare for your beast, the less often it will wake up expecting to be fed. Be ever alert for when you start to worry. Please don't feed the beast.

Transform Your Emotions

Your emotions will turn into actions. If you are paying attention to your emotions, you can direct their transformation. If you are not paying attention to your emotions, they will come out as they are. If you are sad or feeling down, you may naturally stay in bed or avoid people. If you are bored, you may flip through channels on the television, or plod through your normal activities. If you are angry, you may shout at the people around you. If you are happy, you may find yourself singing and dancing. If you are aware of your emotional state, you can consciously transform your moods into action. You can use your moods to create harmony.

You are constantly feeling and acting. You are not always consciously feeling and acting. By recognizing your emotional state, you can be alert to emotional states that prompt you to act in ways that may hurt you or those around you. Anger is an emotion that carries a lot of potential for destruction. If you notice that you are angry, you have a lot of energy to release. It's like you're carrying a lit stick of dynamite. You don't want it to blow up in your hand or around people you love, so you need to take it out to a demolition site to help it knock down the condemned building so that you can build a playground. You need to become creative and use your energy to do something that will make you proud.

    Emotions spur you on to action. That's what they do. With awareness and a little ingenuity, you can change the world. If you are feeling happy, spread joy. If you are feeling sad, create joy. When you learn to transform your emotions to create peace and harmony, you will transform your life.

Truth 2

There Is a Cause of Suffering

If you think that your life's really bad,
Do not blame your mom or your dad.
Watch your anger and greed
And delusion. Indeed,
The three poisons are driving you mad.

Zen Ideas

If you want to use the ideas of Zen to help yourself feel better, there are many ideas that you can use. For example, you can treat everybody you encounter with kindness.

There is the idea that all of your problems stem from your thinking. If you believe that, you should be motivated to change your thinking.

A powerful idea is that enlightenment is possible. There is great comfort to be had in that concept. That means that there is a way out of your suffering.

One idea is that everything is constantly changing. When you apply the idea of impermanence to your mood, you know you will not be stuck in your current mood for too long, because it too changes.

There is the idea that you are perfect as you are, just like Buddha. If you believe that, you will not struggle with self-esteem.

Speaking of self, there is the idea of no separate self. That idea connects you to the entire universe. It is as if your pinky toe had the idea that it is somehow connected to all of the toes on your foot and even to the toes on your other foot. If you understand that idea, then the other Zen ideas will become clear to you.

Any of these ideas can help you feel better if you find them to be true. If you don't want a preconceived idea, just sit and meditate. See what occurs to you. There are millions of Zen ideas to help you feel better, or you can just listen to the raindrops. That is nice too.

You Think You Think

When you think about thinking and think about you, it becomes hard to tell what is thinking and what is you. Are you what thinks or are you what perceives the thoughts? If you think you are thinking, then stop. It is not so easy. As soon as you try to stop thinking all you do is start thinking about not thinking.

If it is not you that is thinking, then you are just observing. You are liking or not liking. You are an enjoyer or a sufferer, depending on what is being thought to you. If liking and not liking is also thinking, then you are a thinker again.

Your eyes see, your ears hear, and you thinker thinks. What is it that knows? Something has to decide which thoughts are right and which are wrong. Something understands what you see, hear and think. Is that you, the knower? It is hard to know anything. Mostly you just think you know things. There you go, thinking again.

It is clear that you and thinking are related. Either you think, or thinking yous (as in the verb *to you*). English doesn't exactly allow thinking to you, so your only linguistic option for you to think.

As your heart beats and your stomach digests, your thinking thinks. What part you play in all of this is food for thought.

The Simple Truth

When life gets complicated, it's best to keep it simple. The truth is the simplest thing there is. Everybody is always trying to tell you what the truth is and that can get confusing. You know the truth. You know what is right. You know how you feel about things. That is the truth.

As soon as you start wandering away from the truth, things start to get complicated. If you pretend to be something that you are not, you are complicating your life. If you tell big or little fibs, you are adding to life's complications. If you talk about people in ways that you wouldn't feel comfortable talking to them, you are tiptoeing around the truth. If you notice yourself in any of these situations, you are becoming aware of your dance with the truth.

The simple truth is what you see and hear. What you think may or may not be true. What you think can be influenced by what you want and fear. The truth exists between what you perceive and what you think about it.

The truth is simple. You like people and people like you. You are a splendid creation. If that does not look like the truth to you, you must be complicating things with thinking.

Logic, Faith, Joy

Logic will only get you so far. If logic were enough, nobody would fall into depression. There's no logical reason to feel so bad about life. When you are depressed, there is no logical way to think your way out of depression. There is also no way to think yourself out of depression without logic. You need a touch of logic to engage your faith. You need to know that there is a needle in the haystack before you commit yourself to looking for it.

A little bit of logic can turn the world on it's head. Something simple like, if years of therapy can make me feel better, then I have it in me to feel better. If antidepressants can change my outlook, then things are not as they appear. If meditation can ease my stress, then my stress is temporary. With a little bit of logic you can understand that there is a way out. From there, you follow faith.

If you have faith that you can make it through the next five minutes, then you have five minutes to turn the world on its head. If you have faith that there is joy in the world, you can observe joy. If you can move your body, stand on your head. There's nothing logical about that, but there could be a glimmer of joy in the experience. Have faith.

Self Pity

If you are prone to self-pity, you should identify more with the self that pities than the self that is pitied. The self that is pitied is the fake self. That is the self that is separate from the universe and at odds with life. That is the self that feels like it is not good enough, that it is filled with flaws and could use improvements. The self that pities is the compassionate self. It is the self that calls for healing, that sees the delusion of the sadder self.

Pity is shy of compassion. Pity is recognizing somebody's sufferings or shortcomings and remaining separate from them. Compassion is recognizing somebody's suffering and understanding their situation as though it were happening to you. If you find yourself trying to pity yourself, then you are one short step away from being compassionate toward yourself. Why indulge in self-pity when you can just as easily indulge in self-compassion?

Taking a moment to indulge in self-pity can be an opportunity for awareness. You can notice the ideas you have about yourself that are causing you distress. When you are aware of your distress, you can call upon your compassion to heal your wounds. Your Self is just fine.

Once you manage to transform your self-pity into self-compassion, you can begin to work your magic on others. After all, we are all part of the bigger Self.

Timing Is Everything

Timing is everything. All of your problems exist in time. When you are feeling sad, scared, bored, anxious or in pain, time becomes oppressive. A new day brings a continuation of your problems. A new day becomes another day of tasks and obligations, a series of chores to endure until you get to a better time. A better time will come and go and come again. Eventually your time will be done and you will die. That's another problem.

Without time, you have no problems. If you are in pain, you can endure pain for this instant. It is the prospect of the pain continuing that makes it so difficult. If you are scared, you are not scared about what is happening now, you are scared about what you think might happen. If you are alive now, death is not a possibility. Death only comes in time.

Even a broken heart only hurts because of time. In the past, you imagined a future that didn't come to pass and that loss hurts. The pain multiplies when the hurt and rejection of the lost love are projected into a dismal future, where the comfort of a different love seems impossible. Without the past and the future, your heart is just fine.

Time is the process of everything changing. The past is done. The future is only potential. Now is the moment of action. When you accept the certainty of the past and the uncertainty of the future, you have no problems. You have thoughts, emotions, and choices. Your problems are a matter of time, not a matter of you. You are fine now.

Beautiful People

You are a beautiful person. I hope you don't have any doubt about that. If you have doubts about that, I hope those doubts are fleeting. If you have lingering, nagging doubts about your beauty, then you must flush your mind.

Worries about your beauty are more about your sense of self than about beauty. You have a self and a Self. Your self is what worries about being beautiful. Your Self is beauty and ugliness and love and hate and past, present and future all in perfect harmony. When your self feels disconnected from your Self, you may worry that you are not beautiful enough.

When you are being your self, you may see beautiful people and want to be them or possess them. You may think that being loved by a beautiful person would fill your soul. You may think that if you were more beautiful, that love would come easy to you. When you are being your Self, you will see a beautiful person and know, that person is also you. In fact, you will see nothing but beautiful people. You will see beautiful people suffering, and you will be filled with compassion and love them with all of your Self.

When you see beauty, whether as your self or Self, that beauty is your perception. You perceive beauty, and that beauty fills you. For that instant that you perceive beauty, you are only beauty, nothing else. It is sad that an instant later the beauty may be squeezed out by envy or longing. If you notice envy or longing interfering with your perception of beauty, then you are your Self-perceiving a beautiful person, your self, suffering. When you notice yourself suffering, don't punish yourself. Treat yourself with love and compassion, as you would treat any suffering, beautiful person.

Holding Happiness

Happiness is our foundation. It is the sea that floats our boat. Happiness is the body beneath our clothes. That is the happiness that holds us. The happiness that we hold is more amusement than happiness. We are happy when we are praised. We are happy when we are entertained, whether it is at the circus, the theatre, or bungee jumping. Circumstantial happiness is different from basic happiness.

When we create, we experience our basic happiness. When others appreciate what we create and they tell us how wonderful our creation is, we experience circumstantial happiness. The basic happiness is always there and available to us, but the circumstantial happiness will come and go with our circumstances. When we try to hold onto our circumstantial happiness we get frustrated. It's like trying to carry an ice cube across a sun scorched desert.

Although it is fun and wonderful to seek circumstantial happiness, it shouldn't be confused with our basic happiness. If we are feeling sad or nervous or disconnected from happiness, then we are focused on our circumstances. When we know our basic happiness is there, we are free to experience all of our other emotions, secure that we can always come home.

Giving Up and Letting Go

It's so spiritual to let things go. It is so pathetic to give up. Giving up implies defeat. Letting go implies acceptance. Letting go is good. Giving up is bad. Letting go is giving up. Giving up is letting go.

Although giving up and letting go are essentially the same thing, there is a world of difference between them. Letting things go is hard physically but easy mentally. It is difficult to let things go, but when we do it, we feel instantly better. Giving up is hard mentally but physically simple. It is reaching the limit of our ability and making a choice to become passive and stop striving. This choice may cause us mental anguish. Giving up is letting go of a goal or an approach to a goal. Letting go is giving up a mindset.

The difference between giving up and letting go is the difference between your True Self and your regular self. Your regular self views your experience through your ego and feels separate from and competitive with your environment. Your True Self is still you functioning as an integral piece of the universe whether you realize it or not.

If you are trying to discover your True Self, you will actively work to let things go and, as you do that, your True Self will be working on backing your ego into a corner until it gives up. Until that happens, when you are faced with a situation where you feel like you should give up, let it go. If you are struggling with letting something go, give it up.

Pass the Rock

If we sit in a circle and pass around a rock, we will each have a different experience of the rock, the circle, and the passing. When the rock comes back to us, we will have a completely different experience from the first time around. It seems natural for us to have a different experience from the person sitting next to us, after all, we are different people. When we have a different experience from ourselves we are also different people. Despite all of our different experiences in space and time, we are also having the same experience. We are all sitting in the same circle passing the same rock. We are one and we are many.

If the rock were happiness, how would we behave in the circle? If each time the rock came to you, you filled with light, would you still pass the rock along? If the rock were sadness, what would you do? What if the rock were happiness when you receive it, but it would transform into anxiety, fear, and sadness as you hold it?

We all carry our various rocks and constantly pass them around. We are in the same circle and we are having the same experience. Yet, from moment to moment, everything is different. Don't let your rocks weigh you down. Pass them around. Share the load. Share the light. We're all in this together.

The Real World

If you don't believe the Buddhist idea that your experience of life is a like a dream, then you must believe that the world that you experience is the real world. If life is just as you think it is, then there is not much room left for mystery. If you don't believe in the idea of delusion, then the world can be a scary place. If you don't think that your state of mind frames your experience, then there is little you can do about your fear except hope you survive whatever it is that is scaring you.

From a Buddhist perspective it is natural not to believe in delusion, that is delusion. A Buddhist who understands delusion will feel great compassion for you if they see that you are scared of what you think is the real world. It is the compassion of a parent turning on a light to keep the monsters away. The monsters live in a child's real world.

Great and immediate comfort comes from embracing the idea that you may be wrong about things. If you believe that, with a different state of mind, you could manage even your current situation, then you can begin to change your mind.

The world you experience is the real world. It just happens to contain delusion. It's time to turn on the light.

Delightful Delusion

There is nothing more delightful than the idea of delusion. We don't like to think that we are wrong within our delusions, but if we are wrong about everything, that's kind of funny. It's like going around looking for your glasses when they're on your face. You can get really agitated wondering where the heck your glasses are, then, when you notice them sitting on your nose, all of your former angst becomes funny.

If you believe in the idea of delusion, that we all might be living in some kind of dream, then you are on the path to waking up from that delusion. You have woken up a little bit. If you follow that path to the point of full awakening, then all of your current problems will become cherished memories.

If you think back to your first crush, you can recall how you were over the moon and under the bus about somebody who you feel completely different, or indifferent, about now. You still enjoy the memory. That crush was a great experience. You are having a similar great experience now. You are immersed in a role that is totally convincing. Play that role with conviction and passion. It is a rich experience you are having. If your experience seems to be draining you, you can explore the idea of delusion and give yourself some space.

Your delusion is a wonderful part of your awakening. Experience it fully, before you wake up.

Consciousness, Intelligence and the Universe

The idea that we are the universe being aware of itself goes against our normal way of seeing things. Generally, we imagine ourselves standing apart from the universe and consciousness is something that we have. Self-awareness is a particularly human attribute. The universe, stars, mountains, rivers, cells and molecules do not have consciousness. Somehow though, the combination of these things make us and we are sort of aware.

Not only are we aware, we are intelligent. Our intelligence stands apart from the universe's intelligence because we consciously create things. If we draw a circle, even a crude circle, perhaps a little lopsided, it is a demonstration of our intelligence. If the universe makes a circle by dropping a raindrop into a puddle or tossing a ring around the moon, it may create a perfect circle, but it demonstrates no intelligence because the universe did it.

We place such a high value on our intelligence that we feel bad if we think we aren't smart enough. We scoff at others who we think are less intelligent. We envy people who can draw better circles than we can. We take pride our creations.

It seems a bit egocentric to think that we somehow possess this intelligence, and that we are the primary source of consciousness. It's fine for our egos to think that. We know better.

One Thing or Another

If it isn't one thing, it's another. That is our suffering in a nutshell. We are all One Thing and we think we are another. When we make an other form what is one, we suddenly stand apart from the world. We have lots of little pieces. There is me and you and we each have a mind and a body, and a self and a soul.

In order to make ourselves seem more like one again, we start to collect things from the world around us. This is me, that is mine. We constantly add to ourselves and become a jigsaw puzzle of our minds, bodies, friends, families, our pasts, our prospects and our possessions. We measure ourselves against each other and, depending on how we measure, we feel good or bad about the results. We become so confused by our separateness, that the idea that we are all part of One Thing is hard to imagine.

When we see one another more as one than other, then we can let go of all the little pieces that we have come to think of as ourselves and just be our Self. When we practice being our big Self, our little problems have nothing to hang onto.

Death Practice

If it were possible to practice death, we would all have tried it once or twice. If we each had a chance to experience death and continue living, we would have a renewed appreciation for life. If we could understand death concretely, we would not fear it looming on the horizon. We would no longer live under its spell. We would not grieve so desperately when others pass beyond. We would also not grieve each setback in our lives. If we had a chance to peek behind the curtain, we would no longer imagine that we are separate from each other.

The world beyond death is not available to us in a preview, so we cling to what we know. We see that if I stub my toe, you don't feel any pain, so we think that you and I are separate. If I stub my toe, I don't feel any pain in my elbow. Even so, I am sure that my elbow and toe are both equally a part of me.

Just as my birth is a part of me, my death is a part of me and you are a part of me. I don't know for certain that a practice death would help us see through the confusion of our lives, but something as large, certain and unknown as real death is enough to contribute to our confusion. We don't have to practice death to free ourselves from death's spell. We just have to practice life. It's all right here. It's alright here.

No-Self Esteem

If you suffer from low self-esteem, it could be a liberating leap to no-self esteem. With low self-esteem, you think that there is nothing special about you. Worse, you may think that you have horrible flaws, or you may actively dislike yourself. This is a self-destructive mindset that only builds on your idea of self. Those ideas need to change. You should take the step from low self-esteem to no-self esteem.

No self-esteem would be not thinking well of yourself at all. No-self esteem recognizes that your existence is sacred, but that it is not all about you. The idea of no self is not that you don't exist. It's that you are not separate from everything else in the world. Your non-self is continuous with the universe. You nourish your body with the air and the fruit of the Earth. You were born from your mother, who was born from her mother, all the way back to the beginning of mothers. You are a miraculous process interacting with light, sound, textures, and temperatures. Your internal world is as vast as the external universe. On top of all that, you have awareness and intelligence.

When you think of your no-self, its hard not to be impressed with yourself. If you think that you could be better, you are wrong. You could be kinder and learn to think nicely about yourself. You are currently performing the miracle of turning light waves into thoughts in your head. You are indeed special. The self that you usually think about is the tip of the iceberg. Your no-self is the iceberg and the ocean.

Believe In Yourself

If you don't believe in yourself, then you believe in yourself. If you doubt your abilities and think that there is something wrong with you, then you must have a strong belief that you exist. You believe in yourself like you believe in the Easter Bunny, even though you may not believe in yourself.

There are those who believe that the Easter Bunny is only a myth, a story to entertain children. These non-believers consider themselves knowledgeable about the world. They think they can discern fact from fantasy. They believe in themselves.

If you believe in the Easter Bunny, or God, or Buddha, or yourself, that is your belief. Some beliefs are right and some are wrong. If you believe in yourself, but don't believe in yourself, then some of your beliefs are wrong. Unless it's the other way around.

Self-Worth

You are valuable and invaluable. You are worth it, whatever it is. There is no doubt about it, you matter immensely. You are worthy. Once you understand that about yourself, you don't have to worry about whether you measure up anymore. Once you stop worrying about yourself, you have nothing to worry about.

If you ever doubt your self worth, there is something wrong with your value system. From your perspective, how could anything be worth more than you? Without you, how could you appreciate anything? Without you to experience it, there is no world at all. That is your real self-worth, you are everything. If you want a rough estimate of your self worth, that is it, you are worth everything.

It's important to place a high value on yourself, because other people may not always recognize your value. They may not see that it matters whether you are happy or sad. In their ignorance, they may purposefully or accidentally make you feel worthless. When you know your ultimate worth, you can quietly sit and demonstrate to the world what you know. You won't worry about whether anybody can see it or not, because you will be busy admiring your view. You won't be looking in the mirror either. You will be absorbed in the wonders of the universe.

What Do You Want?

Think about what you want most in the world. What is it that would make your life complete? What would bring you happiness? Unfortunately, wanting that is causing you pain.

What do you do with your want if you don't want pain? You clearly don't want pain. Unfortunately, not wanting something is also wanting something. Again, that leads to pain. Wanting and not wanting hurts when it is attached to an object. If you want love, that want causes you pain. If you don't want to be bothered that not wanting causes you pain. You are not so bothered by being bothered as much as not wanting to be bothered.

So how do you avoid wanting or not wanting? Good question. How do you avoid pain? Good question. You don't avoid pain. You don't avoid wanting and not wanting. All you can do is notice it all. Notice what you want and notice how wanting feels. Notice what you don't want and see how that feels. Notice your pain and see where it comes from. This is all you can do.

When you don't concern yourself with wanting and not wanting, all that is left is contentment. What more could you want?

The Freedom of Zen

The freedom of Zen is the ability to set down your problems. You can either set down your problems by attaining enlightenment, or, if you can't wait for that, you can do it now. To set down your problems now, you recognize that your problems are a product of your thinking rather than a product of your environment. Although that knowledge may make it difficult to manage your mind, it makes it easier to handle your environment.

Thinking that a problem is real or not can be the difference between crippling anxiety and freedom. If you are faced with a hungry lion, you have a problem with your environment and you need to act accordingly. When you have escaped to safety, if you are still afraid of the lion, you have a problem with your mind, that problem is not real.

Life situations present you with a choice of action. Most of these choices we interpret as problems. The freedom comes when you learn to act without imagining that the situation demanding your action is good or bad. If the lion eats you, you're lion food, good for the lion, bad for you. Problems come when you think the situation is bad and the idea of bad interferes with your action. This applies to all of your problems. You can deal with anything. You are free.

Truth 3

There Is a Cure for Suffering

Acceptance of things now and here,
No matter how bad they appear,
Will open your eyes
And you can realize
That you're perfect with nothing to fear.

Something Possible

Knowing that something is possible is an important piece of information in working to bring that something about. When the Buddha achieved liberation, he demonstrated that liberation is possible. Knowing that liberation is possible is itself liberating.

The belief that it is possible to end your suffering, takes the edge off your suffering. It is only your perception that causes your pain. When you believe that, then you begin the process of questioning your perceptions. See how they create the conditions of suffering with anger, desire and ignorance. Ignorance, in the Buddhist sense, is a belief that we exist independent of everything else.

If you believe that the Buddha achieved liberation, then you also believe in your own delusion. Recognizing your delusion, accepting your ignorance, is a part of your liberation. The greatest part of the Buddha's discovery is that liberation is possible for anybody. That's really something.

Buddha Did It

If Buddha could awaken, then you can too. Knowing that Buddha did it, can bring great comfort. Buddha did it 2500 years ago and countless people have done it since. They all tell us that we can do it too. These people, who have been There, have left all kinds of instructions for the rest of us about what There is like and how to get There.

First of all, There is here. The only difference is perception. When you believe that There is here and you are Buddha, then the mystery becomes, why do you feel like you do? Why can't you see through your delusion? Why does life and death and good and bad seem more important than left and right?

The Buddha You, who has been There, drives you to keep looking. When you know that There is wonderful and understand that There is here, then whenever here does not seem wonderful can remind to look again. The only place you can look is here. Like looking for the ketchup in the refrigerator, you will look with more intensity if know you actually have ketchup. If you suspect that you might not have any ketchup at all you might give up if you don't see it right away. When searching for liberation from suffering, you need to know that liberation is possible. If Buddha did it, It's there, here.

Wild Horses

When you are stuck with an unpleasant feeling, your approach to the feeling can make things better or worse. If you approach your feeling without awareness, you get carried away by it, like galloping off on a wild horse. The horse will take you wherever it fancies and you are at its mercy. If you approach your feeling with awareness, you can watch the wild horses dancing in the fields. The horses can do what they please and you can safely observe their antics.

When a wild horse feels a rider on its back, it will run and buck and try to toss the rider. With feelings, when you get sucked into them, you will feed them by identifying too closely with them. If you unconsciously identify with anger, you will scream and shout, hit things and people and do all kind of things that may hurt others or yourself. You will get bucked around by the wild horse.

If you approach your feeling with awareness, you can see the feeling for what it is, an emotional response in your mind and body. If you observe the feeling, you can learn from it. If you are angry, you can experience what anger feels like. If you don't feed it with repetitive justifications, you can watch it run its course. A wild horse without a rider will not run and buck frantically. If it has a big open field, it will just stand there and graze.

There Is a Cure for Suffering

If you feel yourself being carried away by a strong emotion, take a deep breath and then exhale. Dismount your wild horse and set it free in the open field. You will be safe and the horse will become calm. Then, you can behold its magnificence.

Your Best Friend

Imagine how life would be if your best friend lived your life for you. You would still be you, sitting on a cloud, enjoying a magnificent view. Your best friend would be down on Earth living life. You, on your cloud, would become your best friend's guru. You would have a direct link to your friend's mind and you could give advice as you read their thoughts.

From your cloud, what would you tell your friend when they worry about how they look? What would you tell your friend when they feel like they can't handle a situation? From your cloud, you would fill your friend with confidence and help them to develop amazing habits. You could console them through heartbreak and guide them on amazing adventures.

This is the power that you have over yourself. The only thing that gets in the way is your self. How could you have such confidence in your friend, but doubts about yourself? Find your cloud Self and become your own best friend.

Resistance Is Futile

If you simply accept everything as it is, you won't have any problems. Without problems, you will just do what you need to do. When you have to get out of bed in the morning, you just get out of bed. You may wake up and feel really good, all sleepy and warm under your covers. That is wonderful. You feel good. Knowing that you have to get out of bed should not ruin that wonderful feeling. Resistance may ruin that wonderful feeling. When you think that you don't want to get out of bed, instead of just lying in bed, you are actively not getting out of bed. If you really have to get out of bed, you won't be happy until you are out of bed.

Resistance is what makes a hated task hated. If you don't like to clean the bathroom, but you are disgusted by a dirty bathroom, you can resist cleaning the bathroom until your disgust builds so high that it breaks your resistance. Then, after suffering through disgust, you can suffer through cleaning the disgusting bathroom, hating every minute of it. You have managed to pile suffering on suffering. Without resistance, you notice the bathroom is dirty and you clean the bathroom. Accepting everything as it is does not mean you live with a dirty bathroom. You still clean the bathroom, you just accept that cleaning the bathroom is how you will spend the next 20 minutes of your life. You also accept your hate for that task, so you don't have to think about how much you hate it. You just do it.

Resistance is wishing things weren't how they are. That causes pain. If something seems unpleasant, accept it and recognize that unpleasant is your current experience. It is the only experience you can have. When you see that resistance is futile, you can accept your circumstance. When you can accept each mood as it arises, you accept yourself and you can fully appreciate the present moment, just as it is.

You're So Cute When You're Asleep

You don't need to experience a total, complete awakening to feel better about your life. It is helpful to believe that you have the potential to experience a total complete, awakening. It is also helpful not to concern yourself with experiencing a total, complete awakening. If you believe that a total, complete awakening is possible, then the flip side to that belief is that you are currently, at least partially, asleep.

If you believe that you are asleep in some way, then you can give yourself a break. Look and see how cute you are when you are sleeping. You can treat yourself with kindness and compassion, like you would a small child, and guide yourself lovingly through your slumbering life.

You can also recognize that your friends and family are also asleep. What they think and believe is really important, is not as important as they think and believe, because they are sleeping. You should see how cute they all are in their sleep and treat them with kindness and compassion too.

Once you see that you and everybody else is asleep and cute and you are filled with love and compassion for everybody, you will probably wake up. Then you will see that you are not just cute, but absolutely gorgeous.

When We Were Babies

It is amazing to think that we were all babies. Just before that, we didn't exist at all. As babies, we spent our days in perpetual wonder, experiencing whatever was happening. If we felt discomfort, we cried. If we felt joy, we laughed. Food went into us and poop came out of us. We soaked up love like sponges.

At some point in our lives, we got the idea that we were something different from everything around us. We began to get ideas about what we were and what we were not. We learned who we could and could not trust. We learned that the world was safe or scary. We learned how to negotiate our emotions. We learned that when we do certain things, the world responds in a certain way. Those ideas, formed in our earliest years, remain with us.

These ideas about ourselves and others, life and death, good and bad, formed by child versions of ourselves, with little to no consideration at all, became solid. Now, as older versions of ourselves, we spend our lives defending those ideas with our thoughts and actions. Even though these ideas can cause us considerable pain, we defend them, sometimes to the death.

These solid ideas are not really solid at all, they are just ideas. They are habitual, unexamined ways of thinking. If we practice looking at these

ideas about what we we think we are and we
remind ourselves that we really don't know
anything for certain, we can start chipping away at
those ideas that cause our pain. If we chip
away enough, we may just find our baby mind
again, delighting and despairing without any fear of
the future or regret of the past. If we chip away even
more, we may discover our mind before we were
born. Then we could radiate love like the Sun.

Growing Up

As we grow we change. We gain perspective and lose perspective. When we were children, we had ideas about what we wanted to be when we grew up. What we become when we grow up is nothing like what we thought when we were children. We thought about being things like pilots or doctors or movie stars. We imagined doing fun and exciting things and being admired like the people we admired. How could we possibly have imagined office politics?

When we imagined falling in love and maybe getting married, we imagined having somebody to bring flowers to or to bring us flowers, somebody to hold hands with on the beach, somebody to snuggle. We imagined finding a person who would love us just as we were. In marriage vows, people promise to love each other for better or worse, but what we have always imagined was loving each other better and better. How could we imagine falling out of love?

As children, we imagine worlds of delightful possibilities. When we grow up, we learn to see the world differently. We have to be careful not to forget what we knew when we were children. We were right when we were children. The delightful possibilities are still there. They are mixed in with falling out of love and office politics.

There Is a Cure for Suffering

Growing up means not only imagining who we will become, but noticing who we are. It is also a process of accepting who we are and being who we are. When we become comfortable being who we are, the dreams we had for ourselves as children fade away and we can see the world's delightful possibilities even more clearly.

Life and Death

Life is best appreciated in its relation to death. Like most unpleasant thoughts, we tend to think about death as little as possible. When we ignore death, we lose focus in life. We completely ignore the inarguable fact that we and everybody we love and hate will someday die. Because we ignore this most basic fact of life, we struggle. We worry about what we will wear. We worry about what we have. We worry about how we will find love. We worry about ourselves in every detail of our lives. The fact that we are alive and able to experience the wonder of the world, for a limited time only, is lost on us. If we were able to truly realize our death in our hearts, heads, and bones, our lives would change.

Everybody knows that they will someday die, and that thought can be absolutely frightening. If the thought of death is not frightening, then we are not really thinking about death. We find lots of little things to fear. We are afraid of looking silly to our friends. How can we not fear death?

When you truly examine your death, you will find joy in life. If you consider death and it doesn't lead you to a deep appreciation of life, then you haven't really considered death. You are only thinking about life. Thinking of death, with no romanticism will be frightening. It can also be enlightening.

Born Again Zen

In Zen, every morning when you wake up, you are born again. Also, every afternoon, evening and night is an opportunity to begin anew. In the morning, after a good night's sleep, is a good time to start your next life. You may wake up with worries from your past life, wondering how you will deal with the challenges you imagine for your day. As you transition from the warm womb of your bed into your morning routine you can see your brand new thoughts, and feel your fresh emotions. If you are not full of wonder, then you are habitually living your past life. Fortunately, when you recognize that, you have been born yet again into the present moment. Your grungy mood is in your past.

Each moment you are aware, you can see the world through a baby's eyes, with no separation between what is you and what you see and hear. That is the wonder of being born. As you go about your day, you may forget about your life and die for the bazillionth time. Then you notice your breathing, notice a sudden smell, feel warm or cold, and be born again.

There doesn't have to be anything particularly special about your rebirth, just being aware that you are here and it is now is enough. Happy birthday.

Certain Doubt

Being certain has certain limitations. If doubt creeps in, the bottom could fall out. That's what makes doubt so wonderful. There is no doubt about doubt.

If you fall in love, you don't have to be certain that it is the right love. It is fine to fall in doubtful love. When you are comfortable with doubt and welcome doubt, the doubt becomes more certain than certainty. Doubt is fluid. It recognizes that everything changes. If you demand certainty, doubt drives you crazy. If you want a certain love and you are not loved in a certain way, you will begin to doubt the love, you will doubt yourself and you will become uncomfortable.

If you fall in a doubtful love, you will love just as fully, but you will be open to what happens. When doubt creeps in, you welcome it. The doubts confirm your love, because you are in a doubtful love. You can even doubt your doubts.

If you look for certainty, you will become certain about your fears and your fears will be your reality. When you maintain a certain doubt, you don't have to be cynical, you just recognize that things are not only as they appear. Then you can look with wonder at how they do appear. When you welcome doubt and explore your doubts you fly, because you allow yourself to fall with no ground.

Just Now

When all there is is now, it puts a lot of pressure on now to be something special. Now is clearly something special, but if we demand specialness from now, now may not live up to our expectations. When now doesn't live up to our demands, we start to imagine other times in the past, future or different present, that were better, will be better, or could be better than now.

Those imagined and remembered times may seem better than now, but the remembered times were always leading up to now and the imagined times can only grow out of now. If we think that there is something wrong with now, then our expectations of now are unrealistic. We are making impossible demands of now.

Now doesn't try to impress, but if we pay close attention to all that now is, we can't help but to be impressed.

If you imagine all the activities that are taking place in the world, in the universe and in the cells of your own body right now, you get a sense of all that now contains. If you think of now that way, now seems special. It's nothing special. It is just now.

Imagine Happiness

To imagine happiness you should not fall into the trap of imagining how things should be in order for you to be happy. Don't think that you will be happy when you have the car you want, the house you want, the friends and relationships you want, just imagine being happy with what you have now. There is something within what you have now that is sustaining you and you can find happiness there. If you can't imagine finding happiness where you are now, it will not be easy to find it as your circumstances change.

If you need help imagining happiness, remember happiness. Remember the most recent time you felt happy and the time before that. Remember the last time you felt generally happy. Don't imagine that your circumstances were making you happy. It was all you. Imagine happiness and you will feel happy.

What Matters

The most important thing is what? The most important thing is What. What do I know? What don't I know? What do I think? What is right? What is wrong? What is time? What is space? What are you? What am I?

What we think we know interferes with our ability to know. It is amazing what we think we know. We think we can read people's minds. We think we know what motivates others. We think other people can read our minds. We think we know what is good for us and for them. We think we understand all kinds of things that we don't understand. That is why *what* matters so much. *What* is the wrecking ball that can blast through our jumped-to conclusions.

If somebody tells you something that upsets you, rather than getting angry, you can ask them what they mean. *What* opens the door to understanding. Asking *what* is genuine. If you ask *what* two or three times in a row, you will usually find that the other person doesn't know exactly what they are talking about either.

What is the gateway to the unknown. What's the matter? What is the matter.

Size Matters

Because we have a hard time finding compassion for an ant, that doesn't mean that the universe cannot have compassion for us.

We cannot think that we don't matter just because we are small. We are matter. We matter. That's what we do. If we think that the world is indifferent to us because we are only one of billions of people, that does not make it so. That is just crazy math.

The only way that the universe can show compassion to us is through us. The only way that we can feel the compassion is to accept it. We can notice the universe's compassion through our grandmothers and mothers and fathers and friends, but we tend to attribute that compassion to those individuals. How else is the universe expected to show us that we matter?

The universe provides us with mountains, oceans, volcanoes, butterflies, sunsets and moonlight. That can all feel cold and indifferent if we feel like we don't matter. Even surrounded by all of the universe's grandeur, we don't feel embraced until we get a hug. We can imagine the stars, and the quarks, but it takes something roughly our own size to show us how precious we are. The universe cares. The world cares. People love you. Take the love where you can find it. It's huge and all for you.

Are We There Yet?

We are forever trying to get there, often impatiently. There is a wonderful place. It's the place to be. There is a particular set of circumstances where things are just as we want them to be. The people we want to be with are in the perfect place and we are who we wish we were. We have just what we need there. Compared to there, here can be a little dull.

When we long to be there, we are neither here nor there. As we imagine there, we may approach there, but if we do not also practice being here, then we may not even notice when we get there. By the time we get there, we will be busy looking to the next there.

If we ever want to get there, we have to practice being here. When we get really good at being here, we will find ourselves there. Here.

It Could Be Great

If you ever find yourself suspecting that life is really awful, you have to banish that thought from your head. You need to remind yourself that life could be great. It is important to remember that it doesn't take anything but a shift in outlook to make things better. That shift is mostly not accepting the belief that things are awful.

When you make the slight shift from thinking that things are awful to thinking that things only seem awful, then you are half way there. When you see that things only seem awful, but at a more fundamental level they are ok, then you are well on your way to realizing greatness.

Things feel bad all the time. That is pain. The ability to endure pain and maintain perspective, that is greatness.

Shift Happens

It is a very small shift in outlook that moves you from thinking that your life is not manageable to believing that it is manageable. That tiny little shift can have a huge impact on your life. When you decide that life is manageable, that suddenly makes you completely competent to handle any situation. It puts you in a position to deal with all of your emotions. It helps you plow through your fears with your actions. Making that shift frees you to experience your life.

Once you make the shift it may take some time to test your new idea. It is like walking out onto a frozen lake in the winter. At first you step carefully to see if the ice will hold you. When you see that the ice is solid, you can skate to your heart's content. To carefully test your idea, you recognize whenever you feel anxious or worried and ask yourself what it is that you think you can't handle. Then remind yourself that you can handle anything and move forward.

When you realize that success and failure, gain and loss are all experiences for your enrichment, you are free to act in the moment. The moment will amaze you.

Turning the Tide

I hope you can find a way to feel good about yourself. Then it will be easier to forget about yourself and get on with life.

If you feel bad about yourself, your self is getting in the way. Everything you do gets seen through this self that has all these problems and inadequacies. Every new problem you encounter confirms all the bad ideas you have about yourself and gives you a new reason to feel bad. You may even feel bad for having bad thoughts about yourself. It is not you that is bad, it is the thoughts.

If you notice yourself feeling bad, check to see if you are feeling bad about yourself. Notice if you are imagining problems with yourself. See if you think there is something wrong with you. If you think there is something wrong with you, then you have identified a wrong thought. Get rid of that thought. Remind the thought that you are good. Then get rid of the next thought that tries to diminish you. Bad thought, good you.

When you can see the stream of thoughts that have been undermining your sense of who you are, then you will see that you are not your thoughts. As you pay attention to the thoughts, you can slow the stream, reverse the tide and start to feel good. As soon as you feel good about yourself, you'll notice your thoughts are no longer about you. Your thoughts are about thoughts, activities, behaviors, events, adventures, others. With yourself out of the way, you are free to live your life.

Mind Swap

If we could swap minds, you could pass your mind to me and I could pass my mind to you. We would immediately see our souls. Your memories would be so fresh and interesting to me, I would be fascinated. Of course, I would look into all the dusty corners and painful places. I would be in awe at all you've been through and filled with compassion. That compassion would clear the debris, polishing the shame into acceptance and creating little alters to all the love and joy in your life. Upon receiving your mind back, you would be delighted by the spaciousness. We wouldn't have to speak afterwards, because you would have done the same to my mind. We would have complete understanding. We would probably just look at each other and laugh and laugh.

The sudden ability to swap minds would surely have that kind of dramatic effect. If it were possible to swap minds, we would have been passing our minds around in class as children. We would trust everybody and know that we are all the same. Because we are stuck in our own minds, we don't know how to clean them. We sweep our little messes under the carpet until it becomes difficult to walk. We don't let others in because we are embarrassed by the mess. Your mess isn't so bad. Pass it to me and I'll dust it for you.

The Plunge

If you want to transform your life, you have to take the plunge. You have to commit to the idea that you are worthy. You can think of 1,000 reasons why you are worthy and 1,001 reasons why you are unworthy. When you take the plunge, you don't need any more reasons. You are worthy.

As long as you continue to negotiate this point, you will be standing on the edge and you will spend half your energy worrying about your self. When you take the plunge, you are free to get on with life.

Truth 4

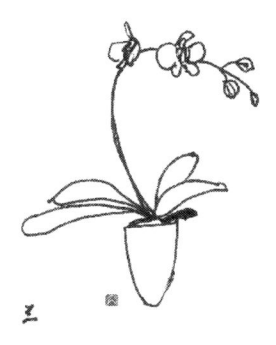

There Is a Way to That Cure

In Zen you examine the mind,
To seek just as much as to find.
In practice you must
Meditate and then just
Be compassionate, loving and kind.

End of Suffering

People don't really take the Buddhist liberation claim all that seriously. If they did, they wouldn't just go about their lives, ignoring the amazing possibilities of the practice. The Buddhist claim is that there is a way to end suffering. That is huge.

Schools don't teach us that if we live our lives in a certain way we will stop suffering. We learn math, literature, science, and music. We learn that if we study hard and apply ourselves, then we can go to a good university, get a good job and we can live a productive life. We just assume that this will make us happy. It may, but it won't end our suffering. To end our suffering we have to pay attention to our suffering.

If we pay attention to our suffering well enough, we will see the cause of our suffering. When we see the cause of our suffering, we will know how to end our suffering and live a happy, harmonious, joyous life. With a payoff like that, it seems worth looking into.

Regulating Emotions

Emotions set the tone of life. They influence actions and behaviors. Actions and behaviors influence emotions. Somewhere in there is consciousness, awareness and us. If we want to regulate our emotions, we have to use our consciousness, awareness and actions.

People usually talk about regulating emotions with respect to children. Part of growing up is learning to regulate emotions. Children's emotions are like thunderstorms, they blow through quickly and intensely. Children's moods spill over into their actions, so if they are feeling bad, they throw temper tantrums. If they feel excited, they will scream and laugh. As we grow up, we learn not to kick and scream so much when our emotions feel intense, but we still get caught up in the ebb and flow of our emotions. Because our moods can last days or weeks instead of minutes, they seem more like personal characteristics than passing feelings.

To regulate these long standing emotions, we use awareness to recognize the feelings and actions to address the feelings. The most basic action we can use is breathing consciously. As we focus our attention on our breathing, we can better see the emotions bubbling away in our minds. As we focus on our breathing and feel our moods, we will know what actions will best address our emotions.

Regulating emotions with our actions is not all

venting and suppressing. It is mostly observing, accepting and then acting with kindness and compassion.

Breathe Deeply

Breathing deeply is the first thing you need to do to change your outlook. A deep breath can reaffirm that despite how everything feels, everything is going to be okay. A deep breath confirms that you are still alive and able to handle the situation in front of you. A deep breath can remind you that you are taking care of your most basic needs and that you deserve peace. That deep breath is a sign of hope.

Sometimes one breath is enough. Sometimes you need several. If you need several, take several. Sit and breathe deeply for five minutes or an hour. Your breath is always there for you. When you notice yourself getting carried away by a mood, take a deep breath or two and let the air out of it.

A deep breath releases the tension you have been holding. Whether you have been holding the tension for an hour, a week, or a year, a single deep breath can be the first step in the transformation of that tension. Any time you notice tension building, that breath is there for you. Irritation, anger, fear, loneliness, can all be addressed with a focused breath. If you remain alert for the onset of these feelings, you can always be ready with a fresh new breath. Whew!!

Two Paths

There are two ways to approach Zen. One is to dance around the fringe and the other is to jump in with both feet.

If you dance around the fringe, you have not bought into the belief that you are living in a delusion. On this path you can use Zen and Buddhism to help combat your neuroses. You can use mindfulness and meditation to help ease your pain and suffering. You can be kind to others and learn to love yourself. In this approach you can wear Buddhism like a beautiful necklace or a crown. That adornment will bring you peace and joy. With this path, you can keep your self and ego and all that you have now.

With the second path, you jump in with both feet. That means that you recognize that you are experiencing delusion and that there is a way to see things clearly. You realize that by following this path you may come to understand that you don't exist as you see yourself today. In following this path, you stand to lose everything. In this path you find a teacher, you join a sangha and you use mindfulness and meditation to ease your pain and suffering. You can practice being kind to others and you learn to love yourself.

The two paths are really one path. The first path is practice without belief, but if you dabble in the ideas, you run the risk of believing them. When

There Is a Way to That Cure

you start believing, you are on the second path. The best thing about both paths is that you get to be mindful, meditate, be kind to others and love yourself. What joy.

Ten Wonderful Things

It takes faith to believe that the universe is wonderful when it feels otherwise. If things feel like they are terrible and that they will never get better, you need to take a leap of faith to get through the day. When you have faith that life can be wonderful, you can use logic to reinforce your faith. Without taxing your imagination, you can think of ten wonderful things about life. If you are willing to tax your imagination a little, you can think of 100 or 1,000.

If you have trouble thinking of wonderful things, you can think about your senses. You can think of ten wonderful smells, ten wonderful sights, ten wonderful feelings, ten wonderful tastes. You can probably think of ten wonderful people, ten wonderful books, ten wonderful songs. If you try, you can probably recall ten wonderful memories. You can even look around where you are sitting and see ten beautiful objects. If you take a break from thinking about all the wonderful things around you, you can take ten wonderful breaths.

When you actively think about all the wonderful things that make up your daily experience, it is amazing that you can fall into depression at all. The world is full of light and love and death and darkness. When you find yourself immersed in darkness, you must have faith that the light is there. The fact that ten wonderful things are within your reach at any time can help to reinforce your faith.

Serve or Observe

When you are feeling anxious, worried or miserable, you have two courses of action. You can either serve or observe your mood.

If you choose to serve your mood, then you feel just as your mood dictates. If you are miserable, you feel terrible about being miserable. You imagine that you will likely be miserable forever. You come up with reason after reason to feed your misery. Your misery, so faithfully served, will remain and continually return to take advantage of your gracious hospitality.

If you choose to observe your mood, you just notice how you are feeling. If you find yourself feeling miserable, you observe your misery. You breathe in and out and see how your misery responds. You remind yourself that the misery is a feeling. It is no reflection of who you are, who you have been or who you will become. You imagine things that might help lift your misery, like calling a friend, going for a walk, or writing a poem. Then you see how your misery responds to your activity. As you observe your mood, understanding that it is only a mood and nothing more, your mood will move on, making room for fresh thoughts and feelings.

If you see your moods as reflections of how things are, you will likely find yourself serving them. If you are feeling anxious, or scared, you will find yourself prone to anger and you will take your mood out on others. If you see your moods as clouds passing through the sky, you can observe them, see what they look and feel like, then watch the sun peek out behind them.

Observing and Serving

It wouldn't be Zen if there were a true choice between observing and serving your moods. If you are feeling miserable and you cry and then take a nap, that may be serving, observing or both.

The difference between serving and observing is in the story you are telling yourself. If you are telling yourself that your situation is impossible, that you cannot handle it and that the world is conspiring against you, if you are finding people to blame for what you are going through and feeling hate and anger, then you are serving your mood without much observing. Observing your mood entails paying close attention to the thoughts associated with your mood and assuming responsibility for creating the change you would like.

Crying is an excellent response to misery. Taking a nap is an excellent response to exhaustion. If you take a nap and wake up feeling refreshed and capable, then you have effectively transformed your mood. Your mood may have been related to your tiredness. When you cry, you center yourself in your body and you release all kinds of tension. When you are done crying, you continue to observe your thoughts. If you think that the crying proves that you were under a lot of tension, then you are observing. If you think the crying proves that you are incapable of happiness, then you are serving.

Observing and serving are constant processes. We are always serving our moods stories. If we observe only the mood and miss the story, then we will just have to take what comes and hope it gets better. If we observe what we serve, we will transform our stories, our moods and our lives.

Big Ideas

Big ideas, like we are one with the universe, or that the present moment is the only reality are just ideas. These ideas, like any conceptual thinking, get in the way of experiencing that Oneness or that Reality. The idea that we should be happy can get in the way of feeling happy. Big and little ideas about how things should be interfere with our ability to experience things as they are. These big ideas, views from beyond, can be helpful in chasing away all the little ideas and motivating practice, but until you can experience the truth of these ideas for yourself, they are just ideas, clouds obscuring the sun.

To experience the possibility of the present moment, you have to actively pay attention to the present moment. See what is in front of you. Notice your breathing. Concentrate on your breathing as though it is the most important thing happening in the world. When you try that, you may experience a sense of peace. If you don't experience peace, you shouldn't imagine that you are experiencing peace, you should see what it is that you are experiencing and keep returning your attention to your breath. If you try this enough, a big idea may occur to you. If that happens, focus on your breath as though it is the most important thing there is.

Mindful Moments

Every moment is an opportunity to be mindful. Your breath is always a good reminder to be mindful because it is always there. Your emotions are also always there. You can use your happiness to be mindful or your fear. The negative emotions are especially good to use because those, we generally try to avoid. Also, negative feelings can inspire you to harm others or yourself. Mindfulness can help you stay with an emotion until it goes away without causing any more problems.

When you are feeling negative emotions, mindfulness can derail your train of thought. Instead of thinking that you are so angry because so and so did such and such, you think, *Wow, I'm angry*. With mindfulness you then notice your surroundings, the sounds, sights, smells and also your thoughts. Each time you think about so and so again you can see how that thought feeds your anger. This may be the difference between punching so and so in the mouth and finding a peaceful resolution to the problem.

Mindfulness is helpful in all parts of your life. Life is filled with amazing, delightful details. Whenever you notice your breath, the sun, the moon, the wind, when you put on your socks, taste your food, or take a shower, these are all moments for mindfulness. When you are mindful, you take a break from the story of your life and live your life. Great things will come.

Liar Liar

It is a sad day when you learn that your most trusted advisor has been lying to you. Unfortunately, this is the case. Your most trusted source of information, you own mind, has been lying to you. It's not all bad news. It turns out that the lies are all kinds of stories about your own deficiencies. If you suspect your mind is lying to you, there is a simple test you can do. Just go look at a mirror and see what your thoughts tell you about yourself. If your inner voice makes you feel inadequate in any way, then you have identified a liar. It's worse than a liar, it's an abusive liar.

Once you realize that your mind's pants are on fire, you can start to look for the truth. If you know a person that lies a lot, the only time that you can trust that they are telling the truth is when they are silent. It is the same with your mind. If you can't trust the noise your mind makes, you have to silence it. The way to silence your mind is to observe it.

Observing your mind is a full time job. You can begin with general observations. If you observe your moods you can get a better understanding of what your mind is doing for you. If you are feeling good, your mind is probably quiet or engaged. If you are feeling anxious or sad, your mind is busy telling you stories and you should pay attention to the running monolog. If you notice your mind passing judgment on others, those you love or strangers, then it is only a matter of time until your mind turns on you and passes similar destructive judgments. Now that you know you mind is prone to fibbing, you will be less inclined to fall for your own baseless criticisms.

If you want to become an expert in observing your mind, you should try a meditation practice. When you sit still and watch your mind, you create a judgment free zone. You can observe the habits of your mind. Watch your breathing and thoughts. When the thoughts carry you away, whether they are kind or cruel, don't add judgment, just return to your breathing. When you learn to observe your thoughts, you will no longer fall for your mind's lies. A quiet mind tells no lies.

Butterflies

Like a net catches butterflies, mindfulness captures emotions. Once you capture a butterfly you are free to examine it. It is the same with emotions. If you cast your awareness around your emotions, you can observe them. By observing your emotions, you transform them.

When you get caught up in your emotions, you become the butterfly, stuck in the net. You don't know why you are stuck, you just know you are stuck. With mindfulness, you examine the net. You recognize feeling stuck. You feel the feelings that are trapping you. You notice that you are in a net. By experiencing the net, you become the net.

With your mindful net, you can catch butterflies all day long. Each thought or emotion that lands on you mind, you can capture and examine. You can make a collection of happy, sad, angry, scared, and joyful butterflies. After examining and appreciating each butterfly, you can release it.

The more you use your mindfulness net, the more joyful butterflies you will capture. As you let them go, feel the freedom.

Hocus Focus

The power of focus is magical. By directing your attention, you can change your world. Just like Cinderella's despair summoned her Fairy Godmother to get her to the ball, you can use the power of your mind to find happiness and fulfillment in your life.

To find happiness with focus, focus your attention on your thoughts. If you are starting from a place of despair, pay attention to the thoughts that are feeding your despair. Watch all of your self-judgments and criticisms. Watch how you tear yourself down by imagining what others are thinking of you. See how you are critical of others. When you focus your attention on your habitual thinking, these thoughts change. As you build your focus, your stray thoughts will no longer pick away at you when you're not paying attention. Happiness rushes in to fill the void left when your mind is not filled with negative chatter.

If you really want to sharpen your magic wand, meditate. Sit for fifteen or twenty minutes a couple times per day. Focus your attention on your breathing, a mantra, a koan, a crystal or a candle. With trained focus you can watch your pumpkin transform into a carriage. With continued focus, your carriage could take you to the moon.

Expect Nothing

Expecting suffering may predispose you to being surprised by feelings of joy. If you expect suffering, you will anticipate suffering and you may suffer from anxiety as you wait for your suffering to occur. Expecting pleasure is no better than expecting suffering, because when you are not feeling pleasure you will feel disappointed and begin suffering. If you don't expect pleasure or suffering, you are left expecting nothing.

When you expect nothing, you are prepared for what comes. If suffering comes, you experience it as it happens. You do not worry about it before hand or concern yourself with it when it is gone. When you experience pleasure, you are happy. If your experience is neither positive nor negative, you are neither disappointed nor fearful. You are just there. There can be quite peaceful.

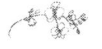

Pleasure and Pain

Pleasure will lead to pain and pain will lead to pleasure. We tend to follow the path to pain by pursuing pleasure. Many follow the path to pleasure by seeking pain. Neither path is the wrong path. Both lead through pleasure and pain. It's just nice to know which path you are taking.

When you do a hated chore, that is taking the pain path to pleasure. People work hard with the idea that if they suffer through their work, they will eventually reap the promised rewards.

When you spend your free time amusing yourself, procrastinating your responsibilities, that is taking the pleasure path to pain. Eventually people's responsibilities catch up with them and they suffer all the more because they are not able to do as they please.

Seeking pleasure is an art. Enduring pain is a discipline. Pleasure and pain are so interrelated, it is pointless to seek one and avoid the other. There is tremendous pleasure in working hard on a difficult task. There is tremendous pain in a love affair.

Whatever path you choose, when you use awareness, you can recognize the pain in your pleasures. You can approach your pain with the confidence that there is pleasure within. The basic path is joyful; pleasure and pain act as your guides.

Feeling the Rain

Working through your negative emotions with mindfulness is like enjoying the rain. Like we try to avoid our stress, we try to avoid getting wet in the rain. If it happens that we get caught in the rain and we give in to being wet, we can find delight in the feeling of being soaked. It can be liberating. We drop our story about how we need to be dry and how uncomfortable it is to be wet and we explore the feeling of the rain on our skin.

That attitude can help get you through a stressful situation. Although you didn't invite the circumstance that brought on your stress, you are in it. When you notice your stress and accept the circumstance, you can give up your story that tells you things should be how they are not. That is mindfulness. It can work with any emotion, in any situation.

It is easy to get rained on and become completely upset about being wet. It is natural to try to wriggle out of our negative feelings and bemoan the circumstances that cause them. Mindfulness is the other option. Feel the feeling you feel. Accept the circumstance as you see it. Be where you are. It can be liberating.

Being Pain

When pain is so great that there is nothing left for you, your only choice is to be pain. When you become pain, there is nothing left to hurt, it is just pain being pain. That is pure acceptance.

If you are so unfortunate as to have to become pain in order to endure pain, then you have already suffered immensely. As you learn to endure your pain with awareness and focus, you can bring yourself to a point where you forget about yourself. There is only the pain, a small pin prick in a vast universe. In order to come to that point, you need to focus your awareness directly at the pain. Don't look left or right or up or down. Your pain is your guide, watch it as though it were a snake poised to strike.

If you focus on the story of the pain or the future of the pain and you wish that it weren't there, the pain will continue to be unbearable. If you enter your pain and become your pain, you will learn its lesson and its wisdom will be yours to share.

Mood Addictions

Our bodies like things as they are. The way that things are includes the chemical reactions taking place in our bodies. We are like living chemistry experiments. We are not just random reactions. We have an opinion about how much of each chemical is in us. When we are feeling good, we have found a good balance. When we are feeling bad, we are out of balance. The problem of being out of balance is that our bodies decide that they like the new normal. Our bodies will inspire us to think thoughts that produce the chemicals that maintain the status quo.

We suffer from addictions. Like our bodies will become addicted to caffeine, nicotine, alcohol, cocaine, or opium, we also become addicted to our moods. Our minds seem complicit in the drug addictions because we willfully use the drugs in pursuit of pleasure. When the pleasure turns into pain, we suffer from the addiction.

Our minds seem to be victims of our mood addictions. We find ourselves in moods rather than actively seeking them. It could be though, that our bodies are seeking the moods. Even though the moods are painful to our minds, our bodies demand their expected chemicals. If we feel uneasy, we think uneasy thoughts and produce uneasy chemicals.

If we are afflicted by negative moods, discipline can help change our body chemistry and produce a new normal. Going for a daily walk, doing daily meditation, eating healthy food are all disciplines you can introduce to change your body chemistry. Mindfulness can also help you notice the steady stream of thoughts that feed your moods. If your body is demanding misery, you can notice when you are feeding it with miserable thoughts.

Take care of your body like a loving parent. It just wants to resist change. When change is needed, use kind and compassionate discipline to introduce new healthy habits.

Rethinking Relapse and Recovery

We all can learn from the world of addictions and mental health as we rethink the ideas of relapse and recovery. People familiar with mental health practices recognize that relapse is a part of recovery, but there still remains a lot of shame in a relapses. Relapses seem like setbacks in recoveries. The idea of recovery is overrated too. What are we trying to recover? Are we looking to get back to some state before problems existed? If that is the case, then we are looking at reawakening.

When we relapse on the road to recovery, we have actually taken a step forward. If we have been accumulating skills, knowledge and awareness and we engage in a harmful habit that we've been trying to break, we have put our training to the test. The skills and knowledge that don't work for us can be rethought. When we learn what works we can teach others our tricks.

When the Buddha experienced enlightenment, he spent the rest of his life becoming enlightened again and again, to help others see the Way. As we continue on our life journey, we can relapse, recover, rethink and discover. In that process, we become beacons to light the Way.

Brainwashing

We all know that brainwashing is a bad thing, but we are all about washing our hands. If you have a dirty mind, perhaps you should wash it. By dirty mind, I don't mean that you think too much about sex, I mean that you are distressed because of your thoughts. Meditation is a good way to rinse your mind, if not actually wash your brain. If you wake up in the morning worrying about your day, 20 minutes of meditation could make all the difference. If you are feeling good in the evening and not particularly worried, meditating for 20 minutes can be delightful. You will be refreshed.

To keep your mind clean and fresh, a regular meditation routine is best. Each time you sit and clear your mind of thoughts you wash your worries away. The more you practice, the more polished your mind becomes and the less dust is able to accumulate. Just sit. Don't think. Grow happy.

You are Here

Every experience is an opportunity for mindfulness. When you are lost in the zoo, you can go to an information kiosk and see a map with a marker saying, "You Are Here". With mindfulness, your breath is that marker. Whenever you are getting lost in time, regretting the past or fearing the future, you just need to breathe deeply and remind yourself that you are here. It is also helpful to remember that here is the only place there is and it can be wonderful.

When you feel yourself getting lost in your thoughts, unconsciously filling your body with tension, pay close attention to what you are doing. Breathe in and out and feel the tension ease. Here is only how it is and it can't be any other way. When, you accept that, here is delightful.

Groovy Ruts

Nobody minds being in a groove. Nobody likes being in a rut. The problem with ruts is that they try to predict the future. If you are in a rut, you see that rut extending as far as you can see. When you are in a groove, you don't worry about where that groove goes, because you are feeling good and glad to be where you are. To turn your rut into a groove, you have to see where you are in your rut.

Nothing looks wonderful from a rut, so don't expect things to look wonderful. Don't expect to feel wonderful. Feel what you feel in your rut. See what you see in your rut. In a rut, a lot of what you see will be painted grey. Notice the grey paint. As you look closely at the grey, you will see flecks of yellow and splashes of red. When you see your present clearly, even your rut starts to look a little groovy.

As you look at your situation with open eyes, without expectations or laments, you will see that your rut is also a groove. All rivers lead to the ocean.

Ace in the Hole

If you don't meditate, you can suffer through the ups and downs of life knowing that if things get really bad, you can always start meditating and you will be able to make things better. If things get really bad and you decide that it is time to start meditating, you need to be patient and give your meditation practice some time to start working.

When you first start meditating, it won't make all your problems go away, but it will give you a familiarity with peace. You may not even feel the peace while you are meditating. You may feel it at other times during the day, when you are sitting in class or at work or just walking. When you start to notice little pockets of peace throughout the day, or you find yourself sleeping better at night, you'll see that your meditation is changing your life.

If you want meditation to be there for you when you need it, you could start practicing now. If things aren't quite as bad as they might be, you could try sitting for five or ten minutes a day. You can figure out what cushions you will sit on, where you will sit and you may find a timer to time your sitting. Once you have your space set up, you can find your comfortable position and practice watching your breath. Then you will know that your meditation will be there for you when you need it. When you find that confidence, your practice is already working.

Drunk Meditation

Drunken meditation is not recommended unless you happen to be drunk when the time comes to meditate. This also applies to high meditation. The Buddhist precepts recommend that you not ingest intoxicants. If you do ingest intoxicants, you are probably not strictly following the precepts.

If you have a regular meditation practice and you find yourself meditating drunk, you will gain insight into your drinking habits and into your meditation habits.

Meditation gives you a good perspective on your life. If you have a daily meditation routine, you will learn all kinds of things about yourself. When you truly understand yourself then the Buddhist precepts will follow themselves. Cheers.

There Is a Way to That Cure

Self-Deprivation Meditation

Depriving yourself of things that you like can teach you about how desire causes suffering. The funny thing about desire is that it seems like something that just occurs naturally in us rather than something we manufacture. When we want to take control of our desires, we have to recognize that they are things that we can construct and deconstruct. We deconstruct desires through self-deprivation and acceptance.

If you want to start depriving yourself of something, begin a meditation practice. Meditation is the ultimate practice of self-deprivation. You do it for a set period of time, for as long as you can stand. Set a timer and sit. You sit in silence. You deprive yourself of movement, talking, listening to music, watching television, texting, eating and whistling, while you pay attention to your thinking. In meditation, you learn to see how your thoughts work as you deprive yourself of these everyday habits. As you get more used to those moments of meditation, you find you a basic feeling of peace in the middle of all that deprivation.

Once you can meditate for fifteen minutes a day, or twice a day, then you find you can do anything. You can quit any habit you want. As you quit an unwanted habit, notice your discomfort when you consider going back to the old habit. When you feel the discomfort, remind yourself that the discomfort is caused by wanting, not by not getting. Soon your cravings will go away. Although you may rid yourself of a bad habit, you may be stuck with a nasty meditation habit and an overwhelming desire to help others. Such is life. Accept it.

The Spiritual Grind

The ordinary mind is the Buddha mind. It is easy to be spiritual in a quiet room surrounded by crystals, chimes and Buddhas. It's nice to let your spiritual side shine at yoga or with your sangha. If you are not a nun or monk, there is a lot more of your life to live. How are you spiritual at work or school, or in the grocery store? Zen has an answer for that.

There is no difference between your busybody, daily grind self and your meditating self. The meditation is the relatively easy part of your day. It's just you, your breath and your focus. As soon as you get off the cushion, the difficult work begins. That's when you forget about your spirit and you just go about your day as you.

Practicing mindfulness, when you have other things on your mind, can be difficult. All you can ever do is do what you are doing. All you can ever think is what you are thinking. Adding awareness throughout your day uses the skills you practice in meditation to appreciate the rest of your life. You don't have to flaunt your spirituality, just know that it's there. Know that you're there. Here.

Finding Peace

In order to find peace in your life, you must focus on creating peace in your life. The creation of peace has to be as important as any of your other life goals. Finding love will not create peace in your life unless you look for a love that supports your quest for peace. Acquiring wealth will not create peace if you do not use peaceful means to obtain and use your wealth. If you want peace in your life, peace has to be a part of everything you do.

It is difficult to fight through your day and expect to be peaceful at night. It is hard to bully your way through the week and hope to find peace on the weekend. The times when peace is most needed is when it is difficult to find. When you are feeling scared, sad, nervous, stressed or angry, those are good times to work on creating peace. When you find yourself in conflict with others, it is a good time to create peace. When you are faced with a daunting task, it is a good time to bring peace into your efforts.

Creating peace in your life is a constant process and a skill. The more you practice, the better you get. Even if you never find wealth or love, if you find peace, you have peace. Of course, if you have peace, you also have wealth and love. Peace.

Afterthought

When a monk asked his master, Joshu,
"What's the nature of dog?" He said, "Mu."
The monk then awoke
And uttered a joke,
"A cow could have told me that too."

About the Author

On December 28, 2013, at the Awakened Meditation Centre in Toronto, Ontario, Canada, Zen master Bub-In, received Dharma transmission from his teacher and Zen master, Venerable Hwasun Yangil Sunim, who belongs to the Korean Jogye tradition.

Zen master Bub-In is also known as Peter Taylor. He practiced social work in Toronto for 10 years, where he experienced enough suffering to drive him to a serious meditation practice. He is the author of the blog, Zen Mister (zenmister.com). He currently lives in New Jersey with his wife and daughter.

About the Artist

In the same transmission ceremony, Zen master Hye-Chung received Dharma transmission from her teacher, Venerable Hwasun Yangil Sunim.

Zen master Hye-Chung is also known as Rebecca Nie. She is a professional artist based in Palo Alto California (www.rebexart.com).

About Inroads Press

Inroads Press (inroadspress.com) of Langley, WA is dedicated to promoting accessible and practical inroads into our personal capacities for healing and transformation.

Printed in Great Britain
by Amazon